I AM a BALLERINA AND SO MUCH MORE

Copyright © 2020 by Dayna Davis

All rights reserved. No part of this book may be used or reproduced in any manner whatsoever without written permission except in the case of brief quotations embodied in critical articles or reviews.

Thank you for your purchasing an authorized edition of this book and for complying with copyright laws by not reproducing, scanning, or distributing any part of it in any form without permission. You're supporting the hard work of writers by doing so.

For information contact:

Dayna Davis at www.iamdaynadavis.com

Written by Dayna Davis Illustrated by Nejla Shojaie

ISBN: 978-0-09899554-1-6 (Softcover)

Library of Congress Cataloging-in-Publication Data is available Printed in the United States of America

10 9 8 7 6 5 4 3 2 1

First Edition: September 2020

FOR MY HUSBAND NATE, THREE CHILDREN, NATELIE, NATE, AND ZOIE WHO HAS INSPIRED ME TO BE SO MUCH MORE.

FOR MY MOM VALERIE BOYCE WHO INTRODUCED ME TO FAITH CONFESSIONS AND CHANGED MY LIFE.

FOR MY DANCE TEACHER MISS DEBORAH KIRKLAND WHO BELIEVED IN ME WHEN I DIDN'T BELIEVE IN MYSELF

FOR MY DANCE STUDENTS AS THIS BOOK WAS INSPIRED BY MY LIFE AS A DANCE TEACHER

I Am a Ballerina ... And So Much More

By Dayna Davis

Illustrated by Nejla Shojaie

"Ashley Grace!" called mom. "It's almost time to leave for dance class. Are you ready?"

"*Almost,*" replied Ashley. She spun around to check herself in the mirror.

Leotard...check!
Tights...check!
Shoes and hair... check!
"Time to go!" She could tell her mom was just as excited as she was. "You don't want to be late on your first day."

Ashley Grace raced into the kitchen and spun around so her mom could get a good look at her.
Her mom smiled. "Are you nervous?"

Suddenly, Ashley Grace's smile faded.
"*What if the other kids don't like me?*"
she asked.
"Oh, they will, don't you worry," her mom
replied reassuringly.

At the dance studio, Mrs. Dayna, greeted her at the class door. "Hi, Ashley Grace. Welcome. Have you had a good day?" Ashley Grace was so excited about class, she hadn't thought about anything else. *"Ummm, I think so,"* she stuttered.

"Well, it's about to get even better," said Mrs. Dayna.
Ashley Grace looked back and smiled at her mom who was watching through the window.

Mrs. Dayna asked everyone to sit in a circle on the floor.
"Hi everyone, and welcome. We are going to have so much fun!"
"This is Zoie, our class Ballerina Bear. Everyone will get a chance to take her home, but for now, she'll sit in front of the class and watch everything we do.

So, put your listening ears on
and keep them on
during the entire class.
Once class is over, Zoie will
whisper to me who
she'd like to go home with."
The children smiled and
wriggled with excitement
as Mrs. Dayna continued.

"Before you transform into ballerinas, I want you to repeat our I AM Faith Confession, which we'll say at the beginning of every class.

Does anyone know what a Faith Confession is?"
The future ballerinas shook their heads and replied, "No."

"A Faith Confession is something you say that you either believe or want to believe. You keep saying it until you believe it, and that's what I want for all of you.
Now, if you're ready, clap your hands one time. And if you're really ready, clap your hands two times."
The ballerinas clapped and giggled.

"Now, repeat after me," said Mrs. Dayna.

"I AM STRONG

I AM BRAVE

I AM CONFIDENT

I AM BEAUTIFUL

I WON'T LET FEAR OVERCOME ME

I LOVE ME

BECAUSE THAT'S THE WAY

GOD CREATED ME TO BE."

"That was awesome," Mrs. Dayna said. "When you feel scared or feel like you want to give up because something seems too hard, think of this Faith Confession.
Can any of you think of something you might be afraid of?"
The ballerinas shouted out all sorts of things, like clowns and worms. One child shouted, "Vegetables!" Everyone laughed.

Ashley Grace thought of the things she was afraid of:
the dark, bugs, and needles at the doctor's office.
At the end of class, Zoie the Ballerina Bear
chose to go home with Ashley Grace since she was a good listener. Zoie also thought she seemed so brave on her first day of dance class.

When Ashley, her mom and Zoie got home, it was already bedtime. Ashely did her night routine:
Shower... check!
Brush teeth... check!
Say prayer... check!

When her mom came in to say goodnight and kissed her forehead, Ashley Grace asked, *"Mom, please leave the light on."* It was the same thing she said every night when she tucked her in. But this time, her mom's answer was different.

"Remember the Faith Confession Mrs. Dayna taught you in class today?" Mom grabbed the piece of paper from Ashley Grace's nightstand.
"Let's say it together:

After they finished the Faith Confession, Ashley Grace smiled and gave her mom a big hug.

"You see," said Mom, "God created you to be those things. Whenever you feel afraid, keep saying those words until you believe them. Now, do you still want me to leave the lights on?"

Ashley Grace grabbed Zoie the Ballerina Bear and remembered how brave she was that day in dance class.
"No," she smiled. *"I'M BRAVE!"*
"You sure are princess. Goodnight!"
"Goodnight mom!"

Ashley Grace couldn't wait to let her dance teacher know how she was working on overcoming her fears. She even made up hand movements to go with the Faith Confession and couldn't wait to teach it to her class. When she did everyone loved it.

She told her dance teacher how Zoie the Ballerina Bear helped with her fear of the dark. When she looked at Zoie it reminded her of how brave she was her first day of dance class.

Mrs. Dayna said, "Yes, I am confident that you were already brave and just didn't notice it."

Ashley Grace learned that the courage she needed was already inside of her and that she wasn't just a ballerina,
she was

Strong...
Brave...
Confident...
Beautiful...
Fearless...

And that's the way God created her to be.

The end.

Story Comprehension

Here are some questions to ask your reader now that you have finished reading the story.

1. Do you remember your first day of dance class? If so, how did you feel?

2. Do you think Ashley Grace was more excited or scared on her first day of dance class? Why?

3. What did some of the kids in dance class say they were afraid of?

4. What was Ashley Grace afraid of?

5. Are you afraid of anything? If so, share something you're afraid of and why?

6. What did Mrs. Dayna say a Faith Confession was? (If you don't remember go back through the story to find out what she says.)

ABOUT THE AUTHOR

MRS. DAYNA

Dayna Davis is the owner of Artistic Expressions Dance Company. She was introduced to dance at 13 years old. She loved to do so many things but one day when she had to choose between basketball, tennis, softball or dance. She chose dance. She has experience in Ballet, Jazz, Modern, Liturgical, African and Lyrical dance. Once she was introduced to the world of dance she fell in love and never looked back.

She's performed and choreogrpahed dances since she was 13 and was a member of Henry Ford Community College dance company that led to her audition on her favorite show *So You Think You Can Dance.*
Her lack of confidence she believes costs her a spot on the show. She made it her mission to uplift other dancers dealing with low self-esteem, comparisons and fear. This birthed her own dance company AEDC.

She is known for her interpretive dance choreography, her dream of mulitcultural acceptance, and her Faith Confessions/ Affirmations.

She believes she couldn't have done it without her husband Nate of 10 years and her 3 beautiful children Natelie, Nathan and Zoie she thanks God for their support and for sharing this amazing journey with her.

"I wouldn't be the person I am without them. God has given me this gift and I'm so happy to share it with all of you!
~ Dayna Davis~

NOW IT'S YOUR TURN

With the help of an adult, create your own Faith Confession or Affirmation. Some people call it Affirmation but it's pretty much the same thing. In this book I teach Ashley Grace and my other dancers a Faith Confession I wrote that helps AG on her journey to getting over her fear of the dark. Getting over your fears might seem hard at first and might take some time, but it is possible. Zoie the Ballerina Bear knew AG was brave even before she did. Sometimes the courage we are looking for is already inside of us. How do you show you're brave everyday?

FUN ACTIVITY
CREATE YOUR OWN

With the help of an adult, create your own Faith Confession. Don't forget to use the recipe below.

RECIPE FOR FAITH CONFESSION

Prep Time: 2minutes Total Time: 5-10minutes

Ingredients:
Paper
Something to write with
Extras (optional) Scissors, construction paper, glitter, markers, stickers or anything to decorate your Faith Confession paper with.

Directions
• Begin your sentence with I AM (optional)
• Add a scoop of powerful and encouraging words. For example, Strong or Beautiful/Handsome
• Add a pinch of something you might be afraid and create a sentence saying that you aren't afraid of it. For example, I am not afraid of spiders.
• Sprinkle in the final touch, Your ending. Consider ending your confession with a word that makes you feel good. Maybe even the reason you believe these things. For example, I am a child of God, The universe works in my favor, or even because I said so. Remember this is your confession so make it just right for You.
• Finally, stand up straight, shoulders down, chest and chin lifted. With a strong and sure voice read your Faith Confession.

Make sure to put your Faith Confession somewhere that is most visible to you so that you can say it every day. Don't forget to share what you have learned with family, friends and neighbors. Let's spread the message together.

Made in the USA
Monee, IL
30 July 2021

74581204R00021